Thomas Lawson

The devotion to the sacred heart of Jesus

Thomas Lawson

The devotion to the sacred heart of Jesus

ISBN/EAN: 9783741192944

Manufactured in Europe, USA, Canada, Australia, Japa

Cover: Foto ©Lupo / pixelio.de

Manufactured and distributed by brebook publishing software (www.brebook.com)

Thomas Lawson

The devotion to the sacred heart of Jesus

THE PREFACE.

THe following Sheets are designed to convey a clear and precise Notion of the Nature and Excellency of the Devotion to the sacred Heart of Jesus, and to propose the several Duties and pious Practices belonging to it. The whole will be conducted in a Manner, that will not exceed the Reach of the most ordinary Capacity, and yet contain every Thing that is necessary for the general Information of the Faithful, and for the particular Comfort of pious Souls.

Loquar ad cor ejus, & ab ipso, quod voluero, impetrabo.

I will speak to his Heart, and from it obtain whatever I shall desire.

S. Bonavent. in stimulo amoris.
P. 1. Cap. 1.

THE DEVOTION TO THE SACRED HEART OF JESUS.

PART THE FIRST.

The Nature and Excellency of this Devotion.

THe Devotion to the sacred Heart of Jesus has Jesus Christ himself for its Author; it is he that planned the Project thereof, he explained the Nature of it and foretold its future Progress. The Church has at all Times considered the sacred Heart of Jesus as an Object worthy her Veneration; for whilst she honoured, as she ever did, his sacred Humanity, doubtless the Heart which is the principal Part thereof, must have deserved her Adoration. However this Devotion, tho' ever holy in itself, has not always been solemnized alike. It is only in these latter Days, that the Time appointed by the eternal Decrees of Providence being come, Almighty God was pleased to disclose to the whole World the inestimable Treasures of the sacred Heart of his divine Son. Such ever was the Conduct of God over his Church; from Time to Time in order to rouse and stir up the Piety of the Faithful, he sets up Devotions, which tho' not new in themselves as to the Substance and Groundwork, are yet so in their Solemnity and respective Circumstances. Thus has he established the Devotion to the most adorable Sacrament of the Altar; thus again the Devotion to his sacred Name, to his sacred Wounds &c.

Sacred Heart of Jesus.

But to give a more clear Idea of this Devotion, let us trace it back quite up to its Source, and see on what Occasion it came forth.

In the Year 1680 there lived in the Diocefs of Autun in the Town called Paroi le Monial in the Monaftery of the Vifitation a young Woman unknown to the World but favoured with the moft ftrict Communications with Almighty God, a worthy Spoufe of the fpotlefs Lamb. Her Life was a Series of the moft eminent Virtues, and her Soul was filled with the moft diftinguifhed Graces. For many Years this devout Soul had been inceffantly engaged in the Meditation of the immenfe Riches of the adorable Heart of Jefus Chrift: for many Years fhe glowed with the holy Extafies of a divine and uninterrupted Love at the Sight of its Perfections; fhe had long fighed after that happy Moment, when fhe might fee this amiable Heart known, honoured and loved throughout the whole World. She then little knew that fhe was to be the happy Perfon chofen by

The Devotion to the

Almighty God to bring about this great Work. On a certain Day within the Octave of Corpus Christi finding herself more than ordinarily burning with this ardent Desire, Jesus Christ appeared and spoke thus to her. (*a*) „ You cannot, says he,
„ testify your Love for me better,
„ than by doing what I have so often
„ asked at your Hands; and disclosing
„ his sacred Heart, he said: " Behold
„ this Heart, which has loved Man-
„ kind so tenderly, and spared nothing
„ even to the wasting and consuming
„ itself in Testimony of its Love, and
„ yet in Return I generally meet with
„ nothing but Ingratitude, Contempt,
„ Sacrileges, Irreverences and Coldness,
„ even in the very Sacrament of my

(*a*) As the Church does not pronounce on the Authenticity of this Revelation, or the Sanctity of the Person to whom it was made, in order to conform as we ought, to the wise Regulations of the holy See, we only relate this as an historical Fact, yet so certain and so averred as to challenge deservedly our Belief and Adherence. We speak here as formerly the Faithful spoke of the Revelation of S. Juliana, which gave Rise to the Solemnity of the Feast of Corpus Christi.

Sacred Heart of Jesus. 5

"Love; and still what more sensibly
"affects me, is that I receive this
"Usage from Hearts peculiarly conse-
"crated to my Service. Wherefore I
"demand of thee, that the first Friday
"after the Octave of the Blessed Sa-
"crament be consecrated to a special
"Feast in Honour of my Heart, that
"a solemn Reparation of Honour and
"a publick Act of Atonement be of-
"ferred to it on that Day, and holy
"Communion received with an Intent
"to repair by it, as far as possible,
"all the Injuries and Affronts it has
"received, when exposed on the Al-
"tars, and I promise it shall dilate
"itself to pour profusely the Gifts of
"its divine Love on all such Persons,
"as shall pay to it this Homage, and
"induce others to the Performance of
"the same religious Office.

These are the Words of Jesus Christ himself, and from them duely weighed as from a most copious Spring flow such Truths, as most properly belong to this Devotion, and are the fittest to convey a distinct Notion of the

Nature of it. They will be more fully unfolded in the following Queries.

FIRST QUERY.

What is the Object of this Devotion?

A. THe Object thereof is the Heart of Jesus Christ, an Object of all others evidently the noblest, the holiest, the greatest, the most divine and altogether the most sweet and most amiable that can possibly be conceived. Hence it follows that a Devotion relating to it bears with it that particular Mark of Sanctity, Dignity, Grandeur, Sweetness and Loveliness, which no other can come up to. The Dignity of this adorable Heart arises 1. from its Union with the most perfect and most compleat Soul that ever was, whereof this divine Heart has been the Organ in the Production of its sensible Affections. From this close Union of the Heart with the Soul, that universal Notion among all polite

sacred Heart of Jesus. 7

Nations is sprung, whereby they are induced to pay to the Hearts of great Men after their Death Honours suitable to the Merits of the Soul they were united to. If so, what shall we say of the sacred Heart of Jesus, since it was united to such a Soul? 2. To what a Pitch of Grandeur and infinite Merit is it not raised by its Union with the second Person of the Blessed Trinity? Whatever belongs to the adorable Person of Jesus Christ claims all our Veneration in an infinite Degree; the least Part of his sacred Body, a Drop of his Blood, a Hair of his Head deserves our utmost Adoration. Every Thing that has but touched his sacred Body becomes thereby venerable, as the Cross, the Nails, the Lance, the Thorns. If the Lance, which pierced the Heart of Jesus, is by that very Touch become an Object of Veneration to the whole Church, what shall we say of the Heart itself, which has imparted so much Dignity to the contemptible Steel?

3. A farther Proof of the Dignity

of the Heart of Jesus is taken from the divine Function it was formed for, I mean that of burning incessantly with the purest and most ardent Flames of the Love of God. From the very first Instant of its Production it glowed with that divine and uninterrupted Fire to the last Instant of its mortal Life, and will ever thus burn for all Eternity. By one single Act of the Love of God produced by it, the divine Majesty is infinitely more honoured, than it could possibly be by the united Love of all Creatures even possible during a whole Eternity. How noble then must that Heart be, the Function whereof is to receive continually the Impressions of this sacred Love, and produce the highest Acts thereof uninterruptedly for all Eternity? Hence the Complacency of the eternal Father for this divine Object, since nothing can be more acceptable in his Eyes, than the never ceasing Love of his only Son.

It is plain from all this that we do not mean to honour the sacred Heart of Jesus barely as an inanimate and lifeless Heart, but we consider it as united to the divine Person and as the chief Instrument of the Operations of the most holy Soul that ever was. This undoubtedly was not sufficiently attended to by those who at first seemed to attack this Devotion. They considered the sacred Heart merely as an inanimate Piece of Flesh without Life or Feeling, as a holy Relick purely material without paying any Attention to its Union with the Divinity and to such spiritual and divine Riches as are annexed to it and which impart to it Life and Motion.

SECOND QUERY.
What is the End of this Devotion?

A. WE are to consider the sacred Heart of Jesus under two different Aspects; on one Side as a Heart full of Love and breathing, we may say, nothing but the Salvation of Mankind; on the other Side as a Heart that is offended, infulted and defpifed by unthinking Man, by Sinners void of all Senfe of Gratitude and unaffected by his Love. The Inclination of this adorable Heart to reconcile Man to God and Earth to Heaven muft raife in us Sentiments of the moft ardent Love and Feelings of the greateft Sorrow to difpofe us for a Reparation of the Wrongs and Outrages it daily fuffers. The End therefore propofed by this Devotion, to which the Faithful are earneftly invited, is in the firft Place to honour by frequent Acts of Love and Adoration, and by all Manner of Submiffion and Homage the unbounded Love of Jefus for us throughout the whole Courfe of his mortal Life, but chiefly in the Sacrament of the holy Eucharift, the Sum and Abridgement of all his Wonders, where he ftill burns with the Love of us. In the next Place it is to fhare in his Grief and to make Amends on our Part for thofe many Infults his Love for us expofed him to during his mortal Life, and ftill now expofes him to every Day in the blessed Sacrament, where he is so little loved by Men, so little known, and oftentimes so outrageously abused even by those, who know him.

THIRD QUERY.

What are the Advantages of this Devotion?

A. THey are numberless and unspeakable. We need but look about us, and we shall immediately discover the many singular Blessings it produces in all Hearts. What more beneficial than a Devotion, which so far from being confined to some barren and outward Practices chiefly consists in a constant Study of the interior Dispositions of this ever adorable Heart, and in an uninterrupted Endeavour to model ourselves on it, and transcribe its Virtues into our own Lives; so that in all Things, as far as we can, we should keep an Eye on this divine Object as the Model we are to copy after in each of our Actions.

Do you desire, pious Souls, to attain the very Summit of Perfection? Behold here a safe and easy Road to it. I say a safe Road: In Matters of Devotion nothing is so much to be feared as Illusion. Whatever is uncommon and singular is deservedly to be mistrusted. Now this Devotion steers clear of any such Danger; the Object it honours is of all Objects the most worthy, the Heart of a Man-God; The End it proposes is quite divine; the practical Duties performed therein are agreeable to the Spirit of the Church; and since Jesus Christ speaking of himself, says that he is the Way that leads to Life, and the Gate thro' which we must enter Heaven, how can we fear being misled by penetrating into the most august Sanctuary of his sacred Heart in order to partake of that Fulness of Grace and Sanctity abiding therein as in its Centre? O! how noble, and precious a Sight, how worthy of the divine Majesty must that Heart be, which is modelled on this divine Original! Hence that un-

sacred Heart of Jesus. 13
common Recollection, and that Modesty so conspicuous in the whole Comportment of many fervorous Clients of this Devotion, that Spirit of Mildness and Peace, that Odour of Sanctity, as I may say, which charms, invites and edifies every Body. Again, by this Means the Heart is imperceptibly weaned from itself and from all Creatures; Selflove abates, the Empire of Sin ceases, Faults are diminished, Imperfections redressed, the Soul fills with God, the inward Man is renewed, and acquires every Day an additional Degree of Strength.

It is therefore a most safe and unerring Road to Perfection. But as a farther Matter of Comfort, I must add that it is also a most sweet, easy and pleasant Road, attended by an uncommon salutary Unction, such as must inspire the Love of Virtue, and an answerable Degree of Fortitude to practise it. For if a solid Devotion to this sacred Heart is ever inseparable from an unfeigned Love for our divine Saviour, it is scarce possible to have this warm and tender Love, without finding in it an admirable Store of interior and quite divine Confolation. And whereas the bare Sight of our Saviour's facred Wounds naturally calls up in our Hearts an unfpeakable Confidence in his Mercies, fo the Remembrance, the leaft Thought of his facred Heart creates a certain Degree of Joy, which is eafier felt than defcribed. I appeal to your Teftimony, devout Souls confecrated in a fpecial Manner to this Devotion, what Sweets have you not felt in thofe happy Moments, when Jefus Chrift has admitted you into his facred Heart? What Delights, what Comforts, what Extafies! Were they not a Kind of Foretafte of the Joys of Heaven?

There is ftill another Benefit entailed on this Devotion, and it is this. It is not confined merely to fome felect and privileged Souls, more verfed in fpiritual Matters, and more enlightened than the common. No: it lies within the Reach of all Degrees of People, the unlearned as well as the most learned. The great ones and the Rich of the World have here no superior Advantage over the Poor and those of the common Sort, because it rests wholly on the Dispositions of the Heart, and all have a Heart to give to God, and may find one in Jesus Christ ever ready to receive their Gift. Cheer up therefore, ye afflicted Souls, narrow Geniuses, indigent and forlorn Creatures. You are not allowed to enjoy in this World either the Pleasures of Life or the Splendour of Honours or the Treasures of Wealth, but you may be admitted into the sacred Heart of Jesus Christ, and therein you will find abundantly whatever the World has denied you: happy, if you but know how to improve this great Treasure, where you may provide yourselves with Riches for Time and Eternity itself.

What then remains but that we enter into the adorable Heart of Jesus Christ! He came down on Earth chiefly for this End to bring with him the sacred Flames of divine Love, which ought to fire all Hearts. Let us then throw ourselves into that burning Furnace, to glow with its heavenly Heat; repair into that sacred Asylum, to be under Shelter from all the Dangers of Salvation; to that Spring of living Water, to find Comfort in our Troubles; to that Model of all Virtues, to transcribe them into our Lives; in a Word to that Place of Delights, to commence there our Heaven on Earth.

FOURTH QUERY.

What are the Obstacles to this Devotion?

A. 1. TEpidity, which, as Scripture teaches, bears hard on the Heart of Jesus.

2. Secret Pride ever opposite to Humility the essential Virtue of this Heart.

3. Self-love the capital Enemy to this Devotion.

4. Unmortified Passions. These stifle the Love of Jesus towards us and

destroy the inward Peace and Quiet of the Mind.

FIFTH QUERY.

Which are the Means of acquiring it.

A. 1. TO petition often for it and that with Fervour, because it is the Gift of God, who bestows his Blessings on such, as ask with Perseverance.

2. To communicate frequently. Fire carried in the Bosom must warm, as the holy Ghost assures us.

3. To visit diligently the most blessed Eucharist. This is the Furnace of divine Love, this the Sacrament of the Heart of Jesus. Love is preserved and entertained by Visits.

4. To persevere with Fidelity in our Devotions to the Heart of Jesus Perseverance is crowned and Love the Reward of Fidelity.

5. To have a filial Confidence in our blessed Lady, and a tender Devo-

18 *The Devotion to the* tion to her and the Saints.

6. To procure a great interior Recollection. A Heart opened on all Sides and exposed to a thousand Distractions can never receive or preserve the Love of Jesus, who is only pleased with the Solitude and Retirement of the Heart.

7. To entertain a strong Desire of loving Jesus Christ.

SIXTH QUERY.

What is the Difference between the Devotion to the sacred Heart, and that which is paid to the blessed Sacrament?

A. 1. IT is very great. They differ in their Object, Motive and End. The first is directed wholly to the adorable Heart of Jesus Christ in the blessed Eucharist without any Relation to the other Parts of his Body: in the latter, the Body of Jesus Christ whole and entire as hidden under the

Sacred Heart of Jesus.

Sacramental Species is proposed to our Adoration without any special Reference to his sacred Heart. Again, the Motive of our Devotion to the sacred Heart of Jesus Christ is 1. the infinite Love he bears us in that sacred Heart united personally to the Divinity, and 2. the many Injuries, Affronts and Indignities it receives still in Return from ungrateful Man, especially in the blessed Eucharist: whereas the Motive of our Devotion to the blessed Sacrament, is the infinite Dignity of the adorable Body and Blood of Christ united to the Divinity, and worthy of the Adoration of Men and Angels.

The End proposed in the Devotion to the sacred Heart is to excite us to a special Honour, and Love for that sacred Heart, and to make an Atonement and Compensation, as far as in us lies, for the many Injuries and Affronts offered to the divine Love at all Times, but principally in the Abuse and Profanation of the most blessed Sacrament. This Reparation of Honour is directed to the adorable Heart, as to the Source and Principle of this divine and euchariſtic Love. Now the Devotion to the bleſſed Sacrament is abſolutely independent on the ſacrilegious Indignities committed againſt the real Preſence; and it would equally ſubſiſt in all its Parts if Almighty God had always been worthily ſerved in the bleſſed Sacrament, ſince it would ſtill ever be juſt to pay to the ſacred Humanity under the ſacramental Veils an infinite Honour, Love, Devotion and Gratitude.

THE DEVOTION TO THE SACRED HEART OF JESUS.

PART THE SECOND.

The Practice of this Devotion.

IN general by the Practice of this Devotion nothing more is meant, than the Use of such Means, as are best calculated to render us true Adorers and faithful Imitators of the sacred Heart of Jesus Christ. Now this Practice is both interior and exterior.

The interior Practice consists in the inward Acts of Faith, Adoration, Love, Hope, Confidence, Gratitude and the like. The exterior Practice consists in outward and visible Acts, such as are meant to denote outwardly the inward Devotion. Of this Sort are Prayers, Novenas, Confessions and Communions, Visits to Jesus Christ in the blessed Sacrament, Associations, Confraternities, Fasting, Penances and generally all pious and edifying Acts, which are performed to honour the adorable Heart of our blessed Redeemer. Whereupon it is not amiss to observe, that we must not so rest and depend on these outward Practices, as to persuade ourselves, that if we have but performed them, we have thereby fulfilled all Justice. This would be confining the whole System of Devotion to bare and empty Ceremonies. Much less ought they to be considered as a Claim to Impunity for ones Faults, or as a Security of a future Conversion after having long slighted Almighty God's Grace. This

sacred Heart of Jesus. 23

would be a gross Illusion and a fatal Abuse ever disavowed by all true Devotion. But on the other Hand, because Devotion is misused, it is no Reason why it should be condemned or suppressed; for the best Things are liable to be misused. The Abuse indeed ought to be checked, but the Devotion itself, wholly saintly and solid, should ever be preserved.

These general Notions being once premised, let us now consider in particular the Devotions to be practised in Honour of the sacred Heart of Jesus. Among them, some are to be performed every Year, some every Month, some every Week, and some every Day.

EVERY YEAR.

THE solemn Festival of this Devotion is fixed on the first Friday after the Octave of Corpus Christi. This Day must be sanctified and consecrated to the Love of our blessed Saviour by Prayer, pious Reading, Visits to the blessed Sacrament, and every other

The Devotion to the good Work; and therefore from the very Eve prepare for this solemn Day by some Act of Penance or Charity, in order to prepare your Heart for the divine Grace. On the Festival itself repair to the Sacraments of Penance and holy Communion. In your Confession on that Day accuse yourself, and detest in a special Manner your many Infidelities and Acts of Disrespect towards the blessed Sacrament. Your Communion ought to be performed with so much the more Fervour, as it is intended as a Reparation of Honour and Supplement for the many Negligences and Defects in former Communions. In the Afternoon you shall make a special Visit to the blessed Sacrament, and there make a solemn Act of Atonement to the sacred Heart, to make amends, as much as possible, for all the Indignities it receives every Day in the blessed Eucharist, and for such as we ourselves have perhaps been guilty of.

EVERY MONTH.

BEsides the principal Feast which happens but once a Year, the first Friday of every Month has been consecrated to the sacred Heart. On that Day the Clients endeavour to perform anew either wholly or in Part the religious Duties practised on the Feast itself, as for Instance, Confession, Communion, Visits to the blessed Sacrament, the Reparation of Honour &c.

They consider the first Friday of the Month as a special Festival proper for them. They are not however thereby debarred from attending to their own respective Employments, provided they offer their Work to God for that End.

EVERY WEEK.

THe warm and fervorous Clients of this Devotion who endeavour to procure for themselves a more plentiful Flow of heavenly Graces, are not satisfied with honouring this divine

Heart once a Month: they have moreover consecrated the Friday of every Week to its Honour. On that Day they perform some Acts of Devotion, some good Works, or small Mortifications either interior or exterior in this View and with this Motive, to testify their Gratitude and repair by their Love the Ingratitude of Man to Jesus Christ. Thus we find that in other Devotions besides the principal Festival, particular and privileged Days are kept every Week. Tuesday for Instance is consecrated to the guardian Angels throughout the whole Year, Thursday to the blessed Sacrament, Saturday to our blessed Lady &c.

· EVERY DAY.

THe following Practices are so much the more valuable, as they are more frequent and lie within the Reach of every Body. They are reduced mostly to this: to perform all our daily Actions in Union with the sacred Heart; so that when we pray, we pray with it; when we love, we love with it; when we act, we act with and in it; when we suffer, we suffer with and for it. This is an admirable Art to heap up Treasures of Merits, Graces and Glory. For as there is nothing so noble in the Eyes of the divine Majesty, as the sacred Heart of his Son, so there is nothing more acceptable to him than the Union of our Actions with that adorable Heart. The infinitely holy Dispositions of it make up for the Deficiency of our very imperfect Actions, which thro' this Union are in some Measure divinized.

Think therefore often, devout Souls, on Jesus Christ, and repair to him in all your Wants; advise with him in your Doubts and Anxieties; speak to him of your Troubles and Afflictions, give him an Account of your Thoughts, Designs and Schemes, lay before him your Faults, Temptations and Passions. Beg of him to remedy all your Evils, live in him, breathe for him alone. He will stand you in Lieu of every Thing else, if you but know how to seek all Things in him.

Besides these Methods annexed to certain particular Times, there are others that may be used at all Times. Such are the Reparation of Honour, the Act of Consecration to the sacred Heart, Communions, Visits to the blessed Sacrament &c. Such again are the outward Signs the Clients of this Devotion wear about them, as Pictures, Medals and Scapulars; such in short are the Beads, the Litanies and other Prayers consecrated to the Honour of this divine Heart.

The Act of Consecration to the sacred Heart of Jesus.

O Most amiable Heart of my divine Redeemer! considering thy infinite Love for all Men and for me in particular, in View of the oppressing Grief and other Pains, thou hast endured for my Sins; in View of the most precious Blood thou hast been pleased to shed for my Redemption; in View of the excessive Love thou hast shewn us in the Institution of the most blessed Sacrament of the Altar, and in View of those infinite Perfections, which make thee so amiable; I N.N. do this Day consecrate myself to thee without Reserve for all the Remainder of my Life. I consecrate to thee my Body, my Soul, my Thoughts, my Desires, my Words, my Actions and my Sufferings, desiring thereby to contribute to thy greater Glory. In particular I consecrate to thee my Heart with all its Motions, desiring it may love thee only, rejoice in thee only, and not breathe but for thee alone; and however unworthy the Offering be, thou canst not refuse it, since thou hast asked it of me.

Receive it then, O divine Heart of Jesus; purify it, sanctify it, and inflame it with thy most pure Love, that it may not act but by the Motion of thy Love, nor suffer but for thy Love, grieve only that it loves thee so little, have its only Joy in loving thee much, desire nothing but the continual Increase of that Love, and fear nothing but to let that holy Love relent and be consumed; in a Word, make my Heart like to thee, that by thee and with thee and like thee it may eternally love the Father, the Son, and the holy Ghost. Amen.

THE
PRAYER
OF
S. GERTRUDE.

Hail, O sacred Heart of Jesus, living and quickening Source of eternal Life, infinite Treasury of the Divinity, burning Furnace of divine Love: thou art my Refuge and my Sanctuary. O my amiable Saviour! consume my Heart with that burning Fire, with which thine is ever inflamed; pour down on my Soul those Graces, which flow from thy Love, and let my Heart be so united with thine, that our Wills may be one, and mine in all Things conformed to thine. May thine be the Standard and Rule equally of my Desires and of my Actions. Amen.

THE LITANY OF THE SACRED HEART.

Lord have Mercy on us.
Chriſt have Mercy on us.
Lord have Mercy on us.
Chriſt hear us.
Chriſt gracioufly hear us.
God the Father of Heaven, have Mercy on us.
God the Son Redeemer of the World,
God the holy Ghoſt,
Holy Trinity one God,
Heart of Jeſus,
Heart of Jeſus formed in the Womb of the moſt bleſſed Virgin,
Heart of Jeſus hypoſtatically united to the eternal Word,
Heart of Jeſus Sanctuary of the Divinity,

} Have Mercy on us.

The Devotion to the

Heart of Jesus Tabernacle of the most holy Trinity,
Heart of Jesus Temple of all Sanctity,
Heart of Jesus Fountain of all Graces,
Heart of Jesus most meek,
Heart of Jesus most humble,
Heart of Jesus most obedient,
Heart of Jesus most chaste,
Heart of Jesus Furnace of Love,
Heart of Jesus Source of Contrition,
Heart of Jesus Treasure of Wisdom,
Heart of Jesus Ocean of Bounty,
Heart of Jesus Throne of Mercy,
Heart of Jesus Abyss of all Virtues,
Heart of Jesus sorrowful in the Garden,
Heart of Jesus spent with a bloody Sweat,
Heart of Jesus glutted with Reproaches,
Heart of Jesus consumed for our Sins,

} Have Mercy on us.

sacred Heart of Jesus.

Heart of Jesus made obedient even unto the Death of the Cross,
Heart of Jesus pierced thro' with a Lance,
Heart of Jesus Refuge of Sinners,
Heart of Jesus Fortitude of the Just,
Heart of Jesus Comfort of the Afflicted,
Heart of Jesus main Strength of the Tempted,
Heart of Jesus Terror of the Devils,
Heart of Jesus Sanctification of Hearts,
Heart of Jesus Perseverance of the Good,
Heart of Jesus Hope of the Dying,
Heart of Jesus Joy of the Blessed,
Heart of Jesus the Delight of all the Saints,
} Have Mercy on us.

Lamb of God, who takest away the Sins of the World, spare us, O Jesus.
Lamb of God, who takest away the Sins of the World, hear us, O Jesus.
Lamb of God, who takest away the

Sins of the World, have Mercy on us, O Jesus.

℣. O most sacred Heart of Jesus, have Mercy on us,

℟. That we may worthily love thee with our whole Hearts.

LET US PRAY.

O God! who out of thy immense Love hast given to the Faithful the most sacred Heart of thy Son our Lord as the Object of their tender Affections, grant, we beseech thee, that we may so love and honour this Pledge of thy Love on Earth, that by it we may merit to love both thee and thy Gift, and be eternally loved by thee and this most blessed Heart in Heaven, thro' the same Jesus Christ our Lord thy Son, who lives and reigns with thee in the Unity of the holy Ghost one God World without End. Amen.

O sacred Heart of Jesus overflowing with all Sweetness! to thee we recommend ourselves and all our Concerns, our Friends, Benefactors, Parents and Relations, our Superiors and Enemies: take under thy Protection this House, City and Kingdom: extend thy Care to all such, as lie under any Affliction, and to those, who labour in the Agony and Pangs of Death: cast an Eye of Compassion on the obstinate Sinner, and more particularly on the poor Souls in Purgatory, as also on those, who are engaged and linked with us in the holy Confederacy of honouring and worshiping thee. Bless these in particular, O bountiful Heart, and bless them according to the Extent of thy Goodness, Mercy, and Charity. Amen.

THE REPARATION OF HONOUR TO THE SACRED HEART FOR THE FEAST &c.

O Most amiable and adorable Heart Centre of all Hearts, glowing with Charity and inflamed with Zeal for the Interest of thy Father and the Salvation of Mankind: O Heart ever sensible of our Misery, and ever in Motion to redress our Evils, the real Victim of Love in the holy Eucharist and a propitiatory Sacrifice for Sin on the Altar of the Cross: seeing that the

sacred Heart of Jesus. 87
Generality of Christians make no other Return for these thy Mercies, than Contempt of thy Favours, Forgetfulness of their own Obligation, and Ingratitude to the best of Benefactors; is it not just that we thy Servants penetrated with the deepest Sense of the like Indignities, should enter upon a due and satisfactory Reparation of Honour to thy most sacred Majesty? Prostrate therefore in Body and humbled in Mind before Heaven and Earth, we solemnly declare our utter Detestation and Abhorrence of such a Conduct. Inexpressible, we know, was the Bitterness, which the Multitude of our Sins brought on thy tender Heart; insufferable the Weight of our Iniquities, which pressed thy Face to the Earth in the Garden of Olives, and unsurmountable thy Anguish, when expiring with Love, Grief, and Agony on Mount Calvary in thy last Breath thou wouldst reclaim Sinners to their Duty, and Repentance. This we know, O dear Redeemer, and would most willingly redress these thy Suf-

ferings by our own, or share with thee in thine.

O merciful Jesus ever present on our Altars, and with a Heart open to receive all, who *labour, and are burdened!* O adorable Heart Source of true Contrition, impart to our Hearts the true Spirit of Penance, and to our Eyes a Fountain of Tears, that we may bewail and wash off our Sins and those of the World. Pardon, divine Jesus, all the Injuries, Reproaches, and Outrages done thee thro' the Course of thy holy Life and bitter Passion. Pardon all the Impieties, Irreverences and Sacrileges, which have been committed against thee in the Sacrament of the Eucharist from its first Institution. Graciously receive the small Tribute of our sincere Repentance as an agreeable Offering in thy Sight, and in Requital for the Benefits we daily receive from the Altar, where thou art a living and continual Sacrifice, and in Union of that bloody Holocaust, thou didst present to thy eternal Father on Mount Calvary from the Cross.

Sacred Heart of Jesus.

Sweet Jesus give thy Blessing to the ardent Desire we now entertain, and the holy Resolution we have taken of ever loving and adoring thee after a proper Manner in thy Sacrament of Love, the Eucharist, thus to repair by a true Conversion of Heart and a becoming Zeal for thy Glory our past Negligences and Infidelity. Be thou, O adorable Heart, who knowest the Clay of which we are formed, be thou our Mediator with thy Heavenly Father we have so grievously offended, strengthen our Weakness, confirm our Resolution, and with thy Charity, Humility, Meekness and Patience cover the Multitude of our Iniquities; be thou our Support, our Refuge and our Strength, that nothing henceforward in Life or Death may separate us from thee. Amen.

THE REPARATION OF HONOUR

Proper for religious Persons.

O Lord Jesus Christ, whose Delight is to be with the Children of Men, thou hast chosen to thyself the Retreat of religious Houses, as most agreeable to thee, and as thy Place of Abode, that thou may'st make of them a new Acquisition to thy Love, and Trophy to thy Glory. In this View thou sufferest thyself to be shut up within the Inclosure of these Monasteries; here thou fixest the Tabernacle of thy divine Sacrament, and thy adorable Body stands as a formidable Fortress against all the Attacks of thy Enemies. Thou hast encompassed these sacred Sanctuaries with the sublime

Laws and Precepts of thy holy Gospel as with an impregnable Wall and Rampart. Thou hast erected a Press of thy sacred Blood, and ordered the Clouds of thy Bounty to shower down in Abundance thy Blessings upon them. After this with Reason calling thy Saints and Angels to bear Witness to thy Words, thou saidst: *What is there I ought to have done to my Vineyard, which I have not done? I have waited in Expectation, that it should bear good Grapes, but it has brought forth wild and bitter ones.* Often ah! too often, O my God, those on whom thou bestowest thy greatest Favours, are the very Persons, who of all are least sensible of thy Bounty, who most sorely afflict thy tender Heart, comply least with thy Graces, and force thee to complain with the Royal Prophet: *Had my Enemy spoke Evil of me, I would have borne it with Patience*, but that the Child of my Family, fed at my Table, nourished with my own Substance, that he should treat me thus, should rise up against me, is a Circumstance that highly aggravates the Measure of my Affliction: and where is the Scene? where the Theatre of these Offences, Indignities and Ingratitudes? Where, O Saviour of Mankind, but in those very Retreats, thou hast sanctified by the admirable Example of so many Saints, in the Sanctuary thou hast chosen for thy Repose, under thy own Eyes in the Land of Saints, *in terrâ Sanctorum*, and at the Tabernacle itself, where thou residest in the Presence of thy Angels. Surely thy just Indignation forced from thy Lips *non videbit*, he shall not see the Glory of God . . .

But stop a Moment, O Lord God of my Salvation, for Mercy Sake withold thy Hand, suspend thy Justice! Hear favourably the worst of thy Servants, who in his own and in the Name of all other Religious presents thee this Day with a Reparation of Honour for all the Tepidity, Sloth, Irreverence and Contempt, with which we have appeared before and approached thy sacred Heart in the blessed Eucharist:

Sacred Heart of Jesus. 43

for all the Communions made out of Custom, Ostentation, and vain Glory. We have displeased thee by bringing a wordly Spirit, a Spirit of Self-ease and Indulgence into Religion; we have profaned these holy Sanctuaries by the Liberties we have given our Senses, the Irregularities we have practised, the Ambition and Envy we have given ourselves up to. We have offended thee in thy own House and under thy very Eyes. We are astonished at ourselves: we are confounded. Oh! that our Grief was as great as the Sea, and our Eyes changed into two running Streams of Blood, that we might ever bewail the Abuses and Injustices of our former Life; grant us, sweet Jesus, a lively Faith, that we may be sensible of the wrong Conduct we have hitherto pursued: give us a true Love of thy Bounty, by which we may become superior to all private and Self-interest, and a Zeal for thy Honour, that we may atone for past Trespasses, and become worthy of thy Favours and Blessings; grant us that Unction and Sweetness, which thy sacred Heart inspires into the Souls of those, who truly love and serve thee. Amen.

THE BEADS

OR LITTLE ROSARY

OF THE

SACRED HEART.

THis little Rosary consists of a small Cross and thirty eight Beads, that is, five of a larger Size to remind us of the sacred Wounds of our blessed Saviour, and thirty three of a smaller Form answering to the Number of Years he spent on Earth in the great Work of our Redemption.

Range the whole thus. The Cross stands in the Front or first Place; then follow three of the smaller Beads shut up between two larger. After which are three Tens or Decades of small Beads, each Decade terminated with a large one.

On the little Cross.

O Jesus! give us thy Heart as a Pledge of thy Love, and as a Place of Refuge, that we may find therein a secure Repose during our Life, and a sweet Comfort at the Hour of our Death. Amen.

On the great Beads.

Thee I adore, praise and love, O sacred Heart of my dear Jesus: penetrated with Grief at the Thought of so many Offences, which have been hitherto committed against thee in the most holy Sacrament of the Altar, I offer up to thee the most amiable Heart of thy most beloved Mother with the Merits of the Saints in Satisfaction thereof. Amen.

On the smaller Beads.

O Sacred Heart of Jesus burning with the Love of us, inflame our Hearts with the Love of thee.

A PRAYER
TO THE
ETERNAL FATHER.

O Eternal Father! let me offer up unto thy Mercy the sacred Heart of thy well beloved Son, even as he offered up himself a Sacrifice to thy Justice. Accept in my Behalf all the Desires, Sentiments, Affections, Motions, and all the Actions of this sacred Heart: they are mine, because it was immolated for me; they are mine, because for the future I am resolved to possess nothing but what is peculiar to it. Receive then the Merits of this sacred Heart in Satisfaction for my Sins, and in Thanksgiving for the Benefits conferred upon me. Receive them, O Lord, as so many Motives of granting thy Servant those peculiar Graces he stands in need of, but particularly the Gift of final Perseverance. Receive them as so many

Acts of Love, Adoration and Praise, which I now offer to thy divine Majesty. This sacred Heart, this Heart only can love, honour and glorify thee, as thou deservest to be loved, honoured and glorified. Amen.

A PRACTICE

For the Visits to the

SACRED HEART.

THis is a most holy and beneficial Practice. It is in these Visits that Jesus himself speaks to our Hearts; it is there he pours on us his most exquisite Graces, enriches us with his true Treasures, teaches us true Science, the Science of Salvation, the Science of Saints. One single Visit is sufficient to change a Soul thoroughly, and convert it.

It is a Matter of just Wonder, that the Princes of this World should every Day be surrounded with a Crowd of Courtiers and Attendants, whilst the

The Devotion to the King of Heaven, the supreme Lord and Master of the World, who is so good as to abide in our Churches for the Love of Men, is there alone and unattended.

Go then to him as to the best of Fathers, the most generous of Kings, the most liberal of Masters and the most tender of Friends, who ardently desires you should apply to him for Favours, that he may have the Pleasure to grant them.

In one of these Visits, you may perform the Reparation of Honour, as above; in another, you may renew the Act of Consecration of yourself, and your solemn Protestation to be eternally his; in others, the different Acts of Love, Adoration, Atonement, Thanksgiving &c.

When from Want of Leisure you are hindered from remaining long with him, offer him your Heart at least; leave it as a Depositum at the Foot of the Cross; unite it to the Heart of that God of Love, who resides on the Altar, as on the Throne of his Mercies, to admit our Adoration and diftribute his Grace.

Holy Communion.

THe devout Client of the facred Heart finding himfelf wholly furrounded with the Bounties of this amiable Saviour, and fired with the Love of him, pants moft ardently after the clofeft Union with him, and ever fighs after the Happinefs to enjoy him. Repair then, devout Soul, to holy Communion; go thither with a View to honour and glorify this divine Heart, to obtain the Graces neceffary to keep you from Sin, to practife Virtue and to attain to that Degree of Sanctity, Almighty God means to raife you to. Afk all thefe Graces with Confidence, fays S. Bonaventure. Can he deny you any thing, who imparts his own felf to you?

When the happy Moment draws near, in which you are about to receive holy Communion, imagine you hear the facred Heart calling on you

and speaking thus to you. " Come to
" me, Sinner, that thou may'ft ever
" renounce Sin. Come, afflicted Soul,
" in order to receive Comfort; come,
" poor and indigent Creature, that
" thou may'ft be admitted into the
" Poffeffion of my Father's Kingdom;
" come, faithful Spoufe, that thou
" may'ft unite thyfelf to thy heavenly
" Spoufe. Then anfwer him thus. " I
" come to thee, moft adorable Heart,
" from the fame Principle, as thou
" inviteft me to thee. I come to be
" filled with the Love of thee, and
" to live by thy Life. I come to lofe
" myfelf wholly in thee and to live
" quite for thee. Behold I open to
" thee the Gate of my poor and wretch-
" ed Heart, open thine to receive
" mine into it. David called thee the
" God of his Heart, be thou the God
" of mine; may'ft thou be the fole
" Mafter of it for ever!

After you have received, imagine
that the Son of God pours down the
Torrent of his Graces into your Soul
to raife it to Life, and fay within

yourself. *It is not I that live, it is Jesus Christ, who lives in me.* Give yourself up therefore wholly to him with all the Warmth you can, and surrender up to him that Heart of yours you have so long and so obstinately denied him, and if you still find some Difficulty in giving it quite up, beg of Jesus Christ, that since he works so many Miracles to enter your Heart, he will please to add one more by changing and converting it.

AN INVITATION

TO A DEVOUT SOUL TO REPAIR

TO THE

SACRED HEART.

ALl the faithful Adorers of Jesus are invited to repair in Spirit every Day at nine o' Clock in the Morning and four in the Evening to his divine Heart in order to make in common some of the following Aspirations.

O moft meek Jefus! make my Heart according to thy Heart.

O divine Heart wounded for Love of us, let us ever be fenfible of thy Bounty, and let thy Love ever plead in our Favour.

We adore thee, O Chrift, oppreffed with Grief in the Garden, and even now defpised by facrilegious and ungrateful Men in the Sacrament of thy Love; for thou alone art moft holy, thou alone art the Lord, thou art the moft high, O Jefus.

Bleffed be the moft adorable Heart of Jefus my God for ever and ever.

No Love, no Heart equals thine, moft loving Jefus.

O may thy adorable Heart be for ever praifed, and all Thanks both in Time and Eternity paid to it.

O adorable Heart of Jefus may'ft thou be known, loved and adored throughout the whole World.

O divine Fire ever burning and never ceafing, raife my Heart into a Flame, that I may always love and never ceafe from loving thee.

Sacred Heart of Jesus.

A PRACTICE
OF DEVOTION

FOR RELIGIOUS COMMUNITIES.

ON the first Friday of every Month, three Religious are chosen to visit the most blessed Sacrament each Friday of that Month, as Commissioners from the Community. They take their Name by Lot according to their respective Commission in this their Charge. The first is called the *Adorer*, the second the *Mediator*, and the third the *Repairer*. The *Adorer* says the Beads of the sacred Heart paying all Homage due to this divine Object. The *Mediator* says the Litany of the sacred Heart in order to obtain for the Community the true Spirit of Religion, and a great Exactness in the Observance of the Vows and Rules. The *Repairer* makes the Reparation of Honour as above mentioned, adapted to religious Houses to obtain Pardon for the Faults, that are daily committed in the Community.

If the Persons appointed for this Duty should be hindered in the Discharge of their Obligation, Care must be taken, that others be substituted in their Place, that the Community may not be deprived of those Graces and Blessings, which God never fails bestowing on each Particular in Consequence of these Visits performed with Devotion and Fervour.

A PRACTICE

FOR A SECULAR FAMILY &c.

THis Practice consists in an Agreement of some pious and virtuous People, of whom one daily at his Convenience visits the Heart of Jesus as ever remaining in the holy Eucharist, and there in his own and the Name of the others his Associates, honours this sacred Heart by the Recital of that Act of Virtue, as hereafter expressed, which in particular has

sacred Heart of Jesus. 55
fallen to his Lot or Choice for that Month. These Acts of Virtue in general are five: *Adoration*, *Thanksgiving*, *Love*, *Atonement for Sin*, and *Petition*.

2. The Number of devout Persons composing it may be greater or less, as Occasions serve. Tho' only five are appointed for the Duty of reciting the five Acts, yet this ought not to hinder every Particular from joining in the daily reciting of the said Acts. Even it is advisable they should, each one for Example choosing that particular Act for himself, which his own Devotion shall suggest.

3. The five chosen by Lot engage themselves to recite daily in the Name of the whole Association the respective Act, which falls to their Charge. They are, if we may call them so, public Deputies or Embassadors to the Throne of Heaven in order to obtain Favours for the rest, and to draw down particular Blessings upon each one of this Association.

4. The Choice of these five Deputies may be made in the following Man-

ner. Let there be as many Billets, as there are Persons, who are to draw for this honourable Preferment: on five only of these shall be written the particular Acts, which are to be said, as the *Act of Adoration*, the *Act of Thanksgiving*, and so on. The other Billets are Blanks. The whole being mixed together, each draws one Billet for himself. Those who draw the Billets written upon, charge themselves with offering up during the following Month to the sacred Heart in the Name of the rest that Act, which has fallen to his Lot.

5. A Draught must be made for the Absent within any competent Distance, and if a Lot or one of the five endorsed falls to any one of them, Notice should be given immediately that no Time be lost, where so great an Interest of the Association is at Stake.

6. This Choice should be made twelve Times a Year, and the most proper Time for it would be towards the End of each Month.

7. Every Associate should have in

Sacred Heart of Jesus. 57

his House or Chamber a Picture of the sacred Heart. The Advantage amongst others is this. Should any Particular be hindered from visiting the blessed Sacrament, he may before this Picture acquit himself of the Obligation he has voluntarily taken upon himself. Jesus Christ has given us an Instance and Proof of how great Merit this Practice is in his Sight. Of this Truth Sister Mary Margaret a great Servant of God is a Witness, as appears in her Life written at large 1729. by Joseph Languet at that Time Bishop of Soissons, and promoted afterwards to the Archbishoprick of Sens. Our blessed Redeemer spoke to her, as is related in the said Life, as follows.

„ I am much pleased in the Devo-
„ tion the Faithful shew for my Heart,
„ and for this Reason I desire the
„ Picture thereof may be drawn and
„ exposed, that by this so amiable a
„ Representation, the Hearts of Men
„ may be softened into Repentance.
„ I promise that such as in a more
„ particular Manner shall honour this

58 *The Devotion to the*
" Picture, shall partake more amply
" of those Graces, with which my
" Heart is replenished.

8. The Virtues of the greatest Estimation, as most dear to the sacred Heart of Jesus, among the Associates must ever be *Meekness* and *Humility*, and the Vices opposite to these must be had in equal Detestation.

If then, devout Reader, this sacred Heart of Jesus is really an Object of your Affections, as no Doubt it ought to be, make up amongst those, with whom you live, your Family, Friends and Domestics a small Association of this Nature, and take my Word for it, Almighty God will look with a propitious Eye both on you, and this your Assembly.

THE ACT OF ADORATION.

Adorable Heart of Jesus hypostatically united to the eternal Word, ever present in the holy Eucharist, receive my Homage and the Tribute of Adoration, which I here bring,

sacred Heart of Jesus. 59
prostrate at the Throne of thy Glory.

May'st thou ever be reverenced and adored by all Creatures; may the raising of Hands, bending of Knees, Prostrations of the Body practised in our Devotions; may the Prayers, Vows and Sacrifices of thy Servants be ever agreeable and acceptable to thee. May the Angels in Heaven ever adore thee, and may the Hearts of all the Faithful, especially that of the most blessed Virgin ever breathe out in thy Honour a most sweet Odour and Perfume of Love, Esteem and Respect.

Sweet Jesus! receive this Act of Adoration. May it be acceptable in thy Sight from my Hands and those of thy Servants of this Association, whom I particularly recommend to thee. Amen.

THE ACT OF THANKSGIVING.

MOst munificent Heart of Jesus hypostatically united to the eternal Word, ever present in the holy

The Devotion to the Eucharist, receive my Homage and the Tribute of Thanksgiving, which I here bring, prostrate at the Throne of thy Bounty.

In the Joy of my Heart I return thee Thanks for all thy Favours. Ye Creatures of God brought forth from your nothing, ye Children of Men created, redeemed and sanctified, praise and magnify your great Benefactor: but chiefly thou, O immaculate and most pure Virgin, preserved from all Spot and Blemish, enriched with the Fulness of Grace, exalted above the nine Choirs of Angels, and next in Dignity to the Throne of God, extol, praise and glorify this munificent Dispenser of all good Gifts. May thy holy Name, O most bountiful God, be ever blessed, may thou be ever praised, and may thy Bounty be ever glorified.

Sweet Jesus! receive these my Thanks. May they be acceptable in thy Sight from my Hands and those of thy Servants of this Association, whom I particularly recommend to thee. Amen.

The Act of Love.

Most amiable Heart of Jesus hypostatically united to the eternal Word, ever present in the holy Eucharist, receive my Homage and the Tribute of Love, which I here pay, prostrate at the Throne of thy Charity.

Be thou ever, O sacred Heart, obeyed and loved by all Creatures, even as Man is always cherished and loved by thee. Thou hast settled thy Affections upon him, and with him thou hast ever desired to dwell. O that I could love thee as thou deservest, and as thou art loved by the Angels and Saints in Heaven, or at least with a Love, if not corresponding to thy Favours, equal however in some Measure to the Greatness of the Obligations, I lie under. Ye Cherubims and Seraphims, ye thrice happy Citizens of the heavenly Jerusalem, and principally thou, O most amiable Virgin Mother, supply by thy Love whatever is wanting to mine. May thy Goodness, O

Jesus, be ever praised, magnified and exalted: May'st thou ever reign as King, Lord, and Sovereign over all Hearts, and may thy amiable Heart draw all Hearts to thee.

Sweet Jesus! receive this Act of Love. May it be acceptable in thy Sight from my Hands and those of thy Servants of this Association, whom I particularly recommend to thee. Amen.

THE ACT OF ATONEMENT FOR SIN.

MOst compassionate Heart of Jesus hypostatically united to the eternal Word, ever present in the holy Eucharist, receive my Homage and the Tribute of Atonement for Sin, which I here pay, prostrate at the Throne of thy Justice.

What have we hitherto been doing, my God? Thou hast bestowed on us most signal Favours even to the Surprize of Heaven itself, and these without any Merit on our Part, even whilst we offended thee; and as thou lovest us beyond Measure, so without

sacred Heart of Jesus.

Measure thou continually heapest thy Blessings upon us. For all these what Return have we made? What Ingratitude have we not shewn? O God of Pity and Compassion! cast the Eye of thy Mercy on our present Repentance, or rather look not on us, look on the blessed Spirits in thy heavenly Court, and especially on the ever faithful Virgin; look on thy devout Servants, who always obey thy Commands, hearken to thy Inspirations, and follow thy Directions. These will interceed with thee in our Behalf, these will atone for our Sins, plead our Cause, and obtain Pardon for past Neglects. These will keep us firm and unalterable in our present Purposes and Resolutions of loving and serving thee more fervently hereafter.

Sweet Jesus! receive this Act of Atonement for Sin. May it be acceptable in thy Sight from my Hands and those of thy Servants of this Association, whom I particularly recommend to thee. Amen.

THE ACT OF PETITION.

MOst bountiful Heart of Jesus hypostatically united to the eternal Word, ever present in the holy Eucharist, receive my Homage and the Tribute of Prayer, which I here offer, prostrate at the Throne of thy Mercy.

To whom, my God, can I address my Petition with equal Confidence? Thy Care watched over me from all Eternity; in Time, thy Indulgence drew me out from my non-Existence; thy Goodness preserves me every Moment of my Life, and thy Munificence supports, feeds and nourishes me. But still, my Lord and Creator, I am environed with a World of Enemies, who continually disturb the Quiet and Peace of my Mind interiorly, and exteriorly assault my Weakness with Violence. I am tempted to cry out a thousand Times in the Day: *Save us, O Lord, we perish.* Open then a Sanctuary into which I may retire, a Refuge, where I may be covered against the Attacks of my Enemies, an Harbour, where after escaping from the tempestuous Waves, I may repose. Thou hast granted the sacred Heart of Jesus unto us, and in it thy Servants have found all these Advantages. The Associates of the sacred Heart have a particular Right and Title to this holy and safe Retreat; give them then a distinguished Place in it. Thou, O Virgin Mother, enforce my Petition by thy powerful Mediation.

Sweet Jesus! receive this my Prayer. May it be acceptable in thy Sight from my Hands and those of thy Servants of this Association, whom I particularly recommend to thee. Amen.

„ The ensuing four and twenty Acts
„ of Adoration to Jesus Christ in the
„ blessed Sacrament may be recited by
„ Way of Reparation for all the Of-
„ fences committed against him by
„ Mankind.

JEsus our Lord and our God ever adorable! O that we could be present in all the Churches throughout the Universe, where thou art not adored as thou ought'st to be, and where thy inflamed Love is not repaid with a Gratitude worthy thy Majesty! we fly at least in Spirit to these holy Places now profaned, and offer on thy Altars there the fervent Love and Adoration of thy holy Mother in Compensation for the Injuries ever done thee by the Jews, by Heretics, and bad Christians. *Eternal Praise be to the ever blessed Sacrament of the Altar.*

2. O Jesus true Sun, that enlightens the Church, and raises into a Flame the Hearts of thy Servants, we adore thee, and to repair the Sloth, Indifference and Tepidity of so many religious Persons, who tho' favoured with the Aspect of so burning a Luminary, remain cold, insensible and inanimate, we offer up to thee all the inflamed Desires of the Seraphims. *Eternal Praise &c.*

3. We adore thee, O eternal Wisdom, and to repair the gross Ignorance, which has caused us to offend thee, we offer up to thee all the Knowledge

sacred Heart of Jesus. 67
of those most enlightened Spirits the Cherubims. *Eternal Praise &c.*

4. We adore thee, O most meek and merciful God, and to repair all the Sins of Anger, Passion and Revenge highly offensive in thy Sight, we offer up to thee the Peace, Mildness and Tranquility of the Thrones. *Eternal Praise &c.*

5. We adore thee, O Sacrament of Love, and to repair all the Thoughts and criminal Desires conceived even at the very Foot of thy Altars, we offer up to thee all the pure Affections and chaste Desires of the Dominations. *Eternal Praise &c.*

6. We adore thee, O immaculate Lamb, that takest away the Sins of the World, and to repair all the Irreverences, Gazing at dangerous Objects, and disrespectful Postures during the Time of holy Mass, we offer to thee the profound Respect of the Choir of Virtues. *Eternal Praise &c.*

7. We adore thee, O Source and Origin of all Sanctity and Innocence, and to repair the Abominations com-

mitted by wicked Priests, who consecrate and receive thee in the State of mortal Sin, we offer up to thee the profound Adoration and Holiness of the Powers. *Eternal Praise &c.*

8. We adore thee, sovereign Lord of the Universe, to whom all Knees both in Heaven and Earth should bend, all Reverence be paid, and in order to repair the many Blasphemies against thy Honour, we offer up to thee the Praises and Homage of the Principalities. *Eternal Praise &c.*

9 We adore thee, Saviour of the World, to whom all Fidelity and Glory is due, and to repair the sacrilegious Communions, and Treacheries of so many false Consciences, we offer up to thee the fervent and faithful Zeal of the Archangels. *Eternal Praise &c.*

10. We adore thee, the Delight of Heaven and Earth, and to repair the Neglect, Indifference and Contempt Mankind shews of that amorous Invitation, by which thou callest them to thy sweet Embraces in the holy Eucharist, we offer up to thee the ready

sacred Heart of Jesus. 69
Obedience, Content, and Happiness of the Angels. *Eternal Praise &c.*

11. We adore thee, never failing Bounty and Goodness, and to repair Man's offensive Diffidence in thy tender Mercy, we offer up to thee the steadfast Reliance and Assurance of the holy Patriarchs in thy Promises. *Eternal Praise &c.*

12. We adore thee, O amiable Jesus, and revere the sacred Mystery of the blessed Eucharist revealed by thy divine Word, taught by the Church and proved by Miracles, and to repair the Doubts Men have had of thy real Presence in the holy Sacrament, we offer up to thee the due Submission shewn by the Prophets to thy divine Oracles. *Eternal Praise &c.*

13. We adore thee, most tender and most amiable of all Fathers, and to make Reparation for the Errours and Infidelities of thy own Children, we offer up to thee the Faith of the Apostles. *Eternal Praise &c.*

14. We adore thee, most loving Shepherd, Pattern of true Charity, and to

make Reparation for the Designs of Revenge conceived in Defiance of thy divine Prohibitions, we offer up to thee the Patience and Prayers of the Martyrs in Favour of their Persecutors. *Eternal Praise &c.*

15. We adore thee, inexhaustible Fund of Treasures, and to make Reparation for all the Robberies committed in thy Churches, we offer up to thee the rich and bountiful Donations of thy devout Servants. *Eternal Praise &c.*

16. We adore thee, O most watchful Advocate, and to make Reparation for the many Negligences of those, who have any Authority in the Church to correct the Abuses and Irreverences there committed against thee, we offer up to thee the exact Attention and careful Solicitude of holy Bishops and Prelates. *Eternal Praise &c.*

17. We adore thee, O God of infinite Majesty, and whom we can never sufficiently adore and reverence, and to make Reparation for all the impious Oaths pronounced against thee, we

offer up to thee the pious Difcourfes made in thy Honour by the holy Doctors of the Church. *Eternal Praife &c.*

18. We adore thee, moft hidden and moft humble Divinity, and to make Reparation for all the Contefts, Difputes, Punctilios of Honour and Scandal, by which thou haft been offended, we offer up to thee the Humility of the holy Confeffors. *Eternal Praife &c.*

19. We adore thee, eternal Prieft, whofe Delight is to offer Sacrifice, and to make Reparation for the Infults and Affronts done to thy Priefts, Religious and Virgins, we offer up to thee thy own invincible Patience together with the true and fervent Zeal of all good Priefts and apoftolic Preachers. *Eternal Praife &c.*

20. We adore thee, true Bread of Angels, and to make Reparation for the Sins committed againft thy Command of Abftinence, we offer up to thee the Fafts and Temperance of the holy Anchorets. *Eternal Praife &c.*

21. We adore thee, O God of all Purity, and to make Reparation for all the Sins, which have hitherto been committed against the Virtue of Purity, we offer up to thee the Modesty and Penance of all holy religious Men and Women. *Eternal Praise &c.*

22. We adore thee, amiable Spouse of our Souls, and to make Reparation for all the Lukewarmness and Indifference shewn by many, particularly in Time of holy Communion, we offer up to thee the Raptures, and Extasies of holy Virgins. *Eternal Praise &c.*

23. We adore thee, most worthy Object of the Love and Affection of Men and Angels, and to repair the Profanations committed in thy Churches by the Effusion of so much innocent Blood, as also to make some Atonement for the poor and indigent Manner thou art entertained there, we offer up to thee the Piety of all the blessed Saints, and the Distress and Want in which thy persecuted Servants were in. *Eternal Praise &c.*

24. We adore thee, Son of the ever

glorious Virgin, and to make a general Reparation, as much as lies in our Power, for all the Indignities thou haft fuffered from Men fince the Inftitution of this adorable Myftery, we have Recourfe to thy holy Mother, looking upon her as under thee, the greateft and moft fecure Refuge of Sinners. *Eternal Praife &c.*

O Queen of Heaven and Earth, Hope of Mankind, who adoreft thy divine Son inceffantly, we intreat thee, that fince we have the Honour to be of the Number of thy Children, thou wouldft intereft thyfelf in our Behalf, and make Satisfaction for us and in our Name to our eternal Judge, by rendering to him the Duties, we ourfelves are uncapable of performing. Amen.

„ It would be advifable to recite
„ over thefe Acts every Thurfday or
„ Friday. Their Number correfponds to
„ the Hours of the day and Night. In
„ each of thefe Hours, the moft amia-
„ ble Heart of Jefus in the Euchariſt
„ is offended and infulted throughout

„ the World. This Recital of the
„ above Acts is a Reparation of Ho-
„ nour we make for such like Offences:
„ nor can it seem too much. However,
„ if on Account of other Occupations
„ it should appear so., fail not once a
„ Month at least, and particularly on
„ the Feast of the sacred Heart of ac-
„ quitting yourself of this Duty. Will
„ you let me, devout Soul, recommend
„ to your Piety another most easy
„ Practice? You have perhaps a Num-
„ ber of Friends, and those equally
„ engaged with you in this holy De-
„ votion. Take to yourself one of these
„ Acts, divide the others amongst
„ your Friends. Let each of them recite
„ daily and offer up to God his res-
„ pective Adoration; nothing can be
„ more practicable, nothing more
„ agreeable to the amiable and offend-
„ ed Heart of your divine Saviour,
„ or more satisfactory for so many
„ Offences daily committed against
„ him.

A MEDITATION
FOR THE FEAST
OF THE
SACRED HEART.

POINT I.

THE HEART OF JESUS IS GREAT AND GENEROUS.

SO great and generous, that the Greatness and Generosity thereof cannot be equaled. No one could ever retire out of the Reach of that Fire, which blazes in the Heart of Jesus. He has extended his Favours to all; he has excepted none. But what Favours? Not only immense Treasures of Grace, but over and above he has given us his sacred Blood, and his Life. He has loved us more than himself, and, which carries his Generosity still farther, he died for his Enemies and his Executioners. He prayed for abominable Deicides, and obtained their Pardon. He bestowed the Bliss of Paradise even on those, who took away his Life with unheared of Violence. No Heart but that of Jesus is capable of such excessive Love. After this, if we are so unhappy as to despise his Favours and his Person, our Hearts must be made of Brass. But, O divine Saviour, I pronounce Sentence against myself. I have experienced how much thou lovest me, and yet I continue almost insensible of thy Love. Monstrous! do I deserve to live! no! take this depraved Heart from me rather than suffer me to have a Heart, that is not wholly thine.

POINT II.

His Heart is Humble and meek.

His Humility appeared on Earth with the greatest Lustre; but his Mercies towards me continue even on the Throne of his Glory. His Heart is also infinitely indulgent. Did not the Guilt of my first Infidelity give thee,

sacred Heart of Jesus.

O Saviour of Mankind, a just Title to crush me like a small Worm of the Earth? And yet thou madest the first Advances to recall me; thou offeredst me a free Pardon and thy former Friendship. Can so meek and merciful a Heart miss a Return of Love for Love? Shall I, O my God, be without Charity and without Meekness? Why dont I impress on mine this adorable Character of thy Heart? *Learn of me, for I am meek and humble of Heart.* Mat. 11. 29.

POINT III.

HIS HEART IS MOST LOVING AND MOST JEALOUS.

O Saviour! thou hast found a wonderful Means never to be separated from me, and to give me incessantly fresh Assurances of thy tenderest Love. Thou hast prepared for me the sacred Food of thy adorable Body, that I may be at Liberty to be intimately united to thee, to possess thee, to enjoy thy Favours and the Caresses of thy divine Love, as often as I can wish. Thy Heart only, O Jesus, could invent and procure these Delights for those, who love thee. But the more loving, the more jealous it is. He will not suffer the least Share of mine to be alienated by any Inclinations to created Objects. What can be more just and equitable? O that I could discover a new Art to love thee with equal Affection! could I penetrate the secret Recesses of thy Heart, and transform my Sentiments into thine, as if both were moulded into one Heart, I would sacrifice my Heart to repair all Injuries done to thine, and I would suffer by Means of thy Heart every Wrong offered to mine.

A PRAYER

FOR THE LIVING AND THE DEAD.

TO thee, O sacred Heart of Jesus! I consecrate the Powers of my Soul with all my Thoughts, Words and Actions. Happy, thrice happy indeed, could they adore, love and glorify thee, as thy eternal Father is adored, loved and glorified by thee. Cancel my Defects, protect me in the Dangers my Life lies expofed to, and defend me in the Hour of my Death. I afk the fame Favour for my Parents and Affociates, my Friends and Enemies, and for all thofe, who labour under the Sufferings and Agony of Death. They have a juft Claim to the weak Intereft, my Prayers may have at thy Tribunal. For thefe I fupplicate, and above all in Behalf of fuch as unhappily lie under thy Difgrace by mortal Sin. May they return to thee, and may they gain the Fruit of fo plentiful a Redemption. I fupplicate alfo in Behalf of the diftreffed Souls in Purgatory that they in their Pains and Anguifh may experience thy Comfort, Tendernefs and Compaffion. This O beloved Heart of Jefus, this is my ardent Prayer, and what I wifh to renew in every Refpiration of my Breaft even to the laft of my Life. Amen.

PIOUS SENTIMENTS

FOR

EVERY DAY.

Angel of God, faithful Friend and Guardian of my Soul and Body! I choose thee to Day as the Executor of this my last Will and Testament, and beg thou wouldst speak for me at the Throne of God in my last Moments, when perhaps I shall not be able to speak for myself. Bear witness at that dreadful Hour, that I believe whatever the holy Catholic Church believes and teaches. Bear witness that I ground my Hopes on the tender Mercy of God, and that I then lay down my Life most willingly, that I may not live to offend him any more. Bear witness that I love him above all Things purely for himself, and that my Desire is to breathe out my Soul in the sacred Heart of his divine Son, and thro' that delightful Passage to enter into the Glory purchased for me by the Blood and Merits of Christ. Bear witness that out of the pure Love of God I hate from my Heart and sincerely detest all my Sins: that I freely pardon such as have any ways offended me, and humbly beg Pardon of those I have any ways offended. Once more, O Angel of God, bear witness that I give up my Soul into the Hands of my Lord and Creator, and that I recommend to his Favour and Mercy the Souls of all and each of my Associates. Amen.

THE CONCLUSION.

ALl that has been hitherto said, all the Reasons which have been brought to explain the Nature, Practices and Excellency of this Devotion, may justly be deemed as so many Motives inducing us to adopt it with Eagerness and Joy; but what includes them all, is the great Delight our blessed Saviour seems to take in it.

Among many Instances that might be given of this Truth, what happened in the miraculous Cure of Nicolas Celeſtini wrought at Rome the 10. of February 1765. deſerves a peculiar Attention. For in the Apparition of S. Aloyſius Gonzaga, with which Celeſtini was favoured, the Saint, after having reſtored him to his Health, directed him to uſe his beſt Endeavours to promote this Devotion, telling him it was a Devotion Heaven much delighted in.

Moreover if any Credit can be given to ſeveral holy Perſons, who agree in affirming the ſame Thing, it has pleaſed the divine Bounty to reveal, that the Church ſhould be indebted for its Tranquility and Deliverance from the Calamities it now labours under, to the adopting the Devotion to the ſacred Heart of Jeſus; ſo that nothing can be wanting to excite our Zeal for promoting ſo ſweet, ſo ſolid and ſo uſeful a Devotion.

THE RULES

OF THE

ASSOCIATION

OF THE

SACRED HEART.

1. THe End of this Association is with the Grace of God to revive continually and nourish in our Souls the Love of Jesus Christ, excited by the Excess of his Love for us. The Heart in general is the most expressive Symbol and Incentive of Love; that of Jesus Christ in particular as under our present Consideration, naturally calls back to our Memory his boundless Charity, and animates us, as much as may be, to a fixed Resolution and Desire of repairing the Outrages committed daily against him in

the adorable Sacrament of the Altar.

2. For your becoming a Member of this Affociation, it is required that your Name be regiftered in the Book, where the Affociation is kept, and that you go to Communion on the Day of your Admiffion in order to gain the Plenary Indulgence granted on that folemn Occafion, and to take up the fpirit of this Devotion by confecrating yourfelf folemnly to this divine Heart.

3. The Affociates fhould be particularly careful and ftudious in frequently uniting themfelves in Mind with the facred Heart of Jefus by Means of repeated Acts of *Faith, Hope, Charity, Contrition &c.*

4. Let no Day pafs without fome Offering or Prayer in Honour of this adorable Heart. One of the following Acts as a Token of your Allegiance and the diftinctive Mark of the Affociation, ought never to be neglected.

„ Adorable Heart of my Jefus! living
„ Source of all Grace and Model of
„ Perfection, fanctify every Moment

"of my Life, and especially that of
"my Death.
"Heart of Jesus! have Mercy on us.
"Heart of Jesus! burning with the
"Love of us, inflame our Hearts with
"the Love of thee.
"May the adorable Heart of Jesus
"live and reign over all Hearts.
"Heart of Jesus infinitely pure!
"grant us Purity of Body and Heart.

5. Every Friday, but in particular the first Friday of each Month should be set aside and appropriated by the Associates as a Day of Humiliation and Atonement to Jesus Christ for the Injuries and Indignities whatsoever received by him in the adorable Eucharist. Some particular Acts of Devotion, as the Reparation of Honour, the Litany, or what else your own Piety may suggest; some small Sacrifice of your Humour, Victory over your Passions, or Mortification may very deservedly be recommended; some Self-denial or Alms may be proper and take place on such an Occasion.

6. All should, if they can conveniently do it, approach the holy Sacraments of Penance and the Eucharist on the Feast of the sacred Heart; on this solemn Festival, beyond the ordinary Prayers on such Occasions, each one should repeat with new Fervour the Act of Consecration to the divine Heart, the Reparation of Honour &c.

7. Besides the above mentioned Communion, two Communions in particular shall be yearly observed; the one in Behalf of the living Members of this Association, the other for the Relief of the deceased Brethren; and in their other Prayers and Devotions they should often remember and recommend to God both this and the other Associations of the sacred Heart, and endeavour all they can to draw on each one a large Share of those Blessings and Graces, which flow continually from this adorable Heart.

8. Finally let every one of this Association make it his chief Business and Endeavour to draw from the sacred Heart of Jesus a most reverential and

sacred Heart of Jesus.

tender Affection towards our dear Lord and Saviour in the holy Eucharist, an efficacious Desire of his own proper Sanctification, and a well governed Zeal and Solicitude for that of his Neighbour united with him in the same Devotion, and under the same Bonds and Rules of Charity, promoting according to his Power, but with Prudence and Discernment, the same holy Practices to the greater Glory of the sacred and adorable Heart of Jesus Christ inflamed with an ardent Zeal for the Honour of his eternal Father and the Salvation of Mankind.

„ Tho' the above Rules and Regulations oblige not of their own Nature under any Sin whatsoever, yet the Associates, we persuade ourselves, will not on that Account be less exact in the Performance of what the Rules prescribe, or less faithful in their Purposes entered upon between God and their own Consciences.

May the sacred Heart of Jesus ever live, be praised and adored.

LETTERS PATENT
OF
AGGREGATION.

We Brother FRANCIS OF S. REGINALD Prior of the venerable Archconfraternity of the sacred Heart of JESUS at ROME.

To our beloved in Christ the Associates of the sacred Heart of Jesus the faithful of either Sex, who are any ways British Subjects, or descend from them, wheresoever they dwell; Greeting in our Lord.

WHereas his Holiness of pious Memory Clement the XII. has by sundry Decrees, namely by one of the 7. of March 1732. another of the 28. February D⁰· and a third of the 12. of June 1736. granted many Favours and Privileges to our Archconfraternity of the sacred Heart; and among the rest has empowered it to unite and associate to itself any particular Confraternity of the sacred Heart extant any where out of Rome, and to impart to it all and every Indulgence, Grant or Release of the canonical Penance due to Sins, that has at any Time been heretofore granted to this our Archconfraternity by his said Holiness.

And whereas a Confraternity of the sacred Heart erected in the Church or domestic Chapel of the English Fathers of the Society of Jesus at Bruges has applied to us thro' its Solicitor in Rome Segnior Joseph Monionelli in order to obtain leave to be thus associated to ours and to share in all its Privileges and Grants: we have thought fit, considering the many good Works of Piety, Penance and Charity performed in that Confraternity at Bruges, (which as to all Essentials is modelled upon the same Plan as ours) to unite and associate it to our Archconfraternity pursuant to the Power given us for this Purpose by the holy See; and we grant to it and its Members all the Indulgences and particular Favours mentioned in the Pope's Briefs, still keeping within the Terms of the Decree of Clement the VIII. which directs such Associations, and Communications of spiritual Treasures.

Moreover besides the Indulgences and special Favours set down in the above mentioned papal Grant, we impart to the said Confraternity a Share in all the Masses, Prayers, Mortifications, Pilgrimages and other good Works performed throughout the whole World by the several religious Orders of Benedictins, Bernardins, Dominicans, Franciscans, Carmelites, Theatins, and Fathers of the Society of Jesus pursuant to the Power we have received thereunto from the Superiors of the said Orders, as may be seen in the authentic Deeds belonging to our Archconfraternity and lodged in our Archives. For the Proof whereof we have caused the present Deed signed by our own Hand, to be underwritten and published by the Secretary of our

Sacred Heart of Jesus.

Archconfraternity, and to be sealed with the Seal thereof.

Given at Rome in the usual Place of our Congregation the 30. of January 1767. in the 9. Year of his present Holiness Clement the XIII. Pontificate formerly our fellow-Associate, and now our most liberal Father and Protector.

Br. *Francis of S. Reginald Prior.*
Br. *Philip of S. Joseph of Callasfantio Secretary.*

Registered. Book the first. Page 63. No. 38.

THE APPROBATION OF THE BISHOP OF BRUGES.

WE permit the publishing of these Letters of Aggregation, still with due Regard to be paid to the

Decree of Clement the VIII. *Quæcumque à sede Apostolicâ*, and we approve of the Choice made by the Associates of the Friday after the Octave of *Corpus Christi* for the principal Feast of the Association in order to gain the plenary Indulgence, and of the first Sunday in Advent, the second Sunday after the Epiphany, the third after Easter, and the first Sunday of October to gain the Indulgences of seven Years and of so many Quarantains or 40. Days.

 Given at Bruges in our Episcopal Palace the 20. of March 1767.
By the Orders of his Lordship the Bishop of Bruges.
  C. Beerenbroek Secretary.

N. B. These Indulgences only regard those, who on the Solemnity of the sacred Heart, and on the above mentioned Sundays shall visit the Church, Chapel or Oratory, where the Association is kept.

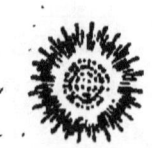

CLEMEMS PAPA XII.

AD PERPETUAM REI MEMORIAM.

CUm, ficut accepimus, in Ecclefia Sancti Theodori de Urbe prope forum Boarium, una pia, & devota utriufque fexus Chrifti fidelium Confraternitas fub titulo Sanctiffimi Cordis Chrifti (non tamen pro hominibus unius fpecialis artis) canonicè erecta, feu erigenda exiftat, cujus Confratres, & Conforores quamplurima pietatis, & charitatis opera exercere confueverunt, feu intendunt; nos, ut Confraternitas hujufmodi majora in dies fufcipiat incrementa, de omnipotentis Dei mifericordia, ac Beatorum Petri, & Pauli Apoftolorum ejus auctoritate confifi, omnibus utriufque fexus Chrifti fidelibus, qui dictam Confraternitatem in pofterum ingredientur, die primo eorum ingreffus, fi verè pœnitentes, & confeffi Sanctiffimum Euchariftiæ Sacramentum fumpferint, plenariam; ac tam defcriptis, quam pro tempore defcriben-

G

dis in dicta Confraternitate Confratribus, & Consororibus, in cujuslibet eorum mortis articulo, si verè quoque pœnitentes, & confessi, ac sacra communione refecti, vel quatenus id facere nequiverint, saltem contriti, nomen Jesu ore, si potuerint, sin minùs, corde devotè invocaverint, etiam Plenariam; necnon eisdem nunc, & pro tempore existentibus dictæ Confraternitatis Confratribus & Consororibus etiam verè pœnitentibus, & confessis, ac sacra communione refectis, qui præfatæ Confraternitatis Ecclesiam seu Cappellam, vel Oratorium, die festo principali dictæ Confraternitatis per eosdem Confratres semel tantum eligendo, & à dilecto filio nostro in eadem Urbe Vicario in spiritualibus generali approbando, à primis Vesperis, usque ad occasum Solis diei hujusmodi singulis annis devotè visitaverint, & ibi pro Christianorum Principum concordia, hæresum extirpatione, ac Sanctæ Matris Ecclesiæ exaltatione pias ad Deum preces effuderint, plenariam similiter omnium peccatorum suorum indulgentiam, & remissionem misericorditer in Domino concedimus. Infuper dictis Confratribus, & Confororibus etiam verè pœnitentibus & confeffis, ac facra communione refectis Ecclefiam, feu Cappellam, vel Oratorium hujufmodi in quatuor aliis anni feriatis, vel non feriatis, feu Dominicis diebus per memoratos Confratres femel tantum etiam eligendis, & ab eodem Vicario approbandis, ut fupra vifitantibus, & ibidem orantibus, quo die prædictorum id egerint, feptem annos, & totidem quadragenas. Quoties verò Miffis, & aliis Divinis Officiis in Ecclefia, feu Cappella, vel Oratorio hujufmodi pro tempore celebrandis, & recitandis, feu Congregationibus publicis, vel privatis ejufdem Confraternitatis ubivis faciendis interfuerint, aut pauperes hofpitio fufceperint, vel pacem inter inimicos compofuerint, feu componi fecerint, vel procuraverint, necnon etiam qui corpora Defunctorum tam Confratrum, & Confororum hujufmodi, quam aliorum, ad fepulturam affociaverint, aut quafcumque Proceffiones de licentia ejufdem Vicarii facien., Sanctissimumque Euchariſtiæ Sacramentum tam in Proceſſionibus, quam cum ad infirmos, aut alias ubicumque, & quomodocumque pro tempore deferetur, comitati fuerint, vel ſi impediti, Campanæ ad id ſigno dato ſemel Orationem Dominicam, & ſalutationem Angelicam dixerint, aut etiam quinquies orationem, & ſalutationem eaſdem pro animabus defunctorum Confratrum, & Conſororum hujuſmodi recitaverint, aut devium aliquem ad viam ſalutis reduxerint, & ignorantes præcepta Dei, & ea, quæ ad ſalutem ſunt, docuerint, aut quodcumque aliud pietatis vel charitatis opus exercuerint, toties pro quolibet prædictorum operum exercitio ſexaginta dies de injunctis eis, ſeu alias quomodolibet debitis pœnitentiis in forma Eccleſiæ conſueta relaxamus. Præſentibus perpetuis futuris temporibus valituris. Volumus autem, ut ſi alias dictis Confratribus, & Conſororibus præmiſſa peragen. aliqua alia Indulgentia perpetuò, vel ad tempus nondum elapſum duratura conceſſa fuerit, præſentes nullæ sint; utque si dicta Confraternitas alicui Archiconfraternitati aggregata jam sit, vel in posterum aggregetur, aut quavis alia ratione uniatur, vel etiam quomodolibet instituatur, priores, & quævis aliæ litteræ Apostolicæ illis nullatenus suffragentur, sed ex tunc eo ipso nullæ sint. Datum Romæ apud Sanctam Mariam Majorem sub Annulo Piscatoris die XXVIII. Febr. MDCCXXXII. Pontificatus nostri anno secundo.

F. Cardinalis Oliverius.

CLEMENS PAPA XII.

AD PERPETUAM REI MEMORIAM.

CUm Nos nuper per quasdam nostras in simili forma Brevis die XXVIII. Februarii proximè præteriti expeditas litteras Confraternitati sub denominatione Sanctissimi Cordis Christi in Ecclesia Sancti Theodori de Urbe propè Forum Boarium sita canonicè erectæ, & institutæ, ejusque Confratribus, & Consororibus nonnullas Indulgentias, ac peccatorum Relaxationes sub certis modo & forma tunc expressis perpetuo concesserimus, & aliàs proùt in eisdem litteris, quarum tenorem præsentibus pro expresso haberi volumus, uberiùs continetur. Et sicut pro parte dilectorum filiorum Officialium, & Confratrum dictæ Confraternitatis nobis subinde expositum fuit, ipsi Confraternitatem ejusmodi Archiconfraternitatis titulo decorari plurimùm desiderent: Nobis propterea humiliter supplicari fecerunt, ut sibi in præmissis opportunè providere, &, ut infra, indulgere de benignitate Apostolica dignaremur. Nos igitur ipsos exponentes specialibus favoribus, & gratiis prosequi volentes, & eorum singulares personas à quibusvis Excommunicationis, Suspensionis, & Interdicti, aliisque Ecclesiasticis Sententiis, Censuris, & pœnis à Jure, vel ab homine quavis occasione, vel causa latis, si quibus quomodolibet innodatæ existunt, ad effectum præsentium dumtaxat consequentium harum serie absolventes, & absolutas fore censentes, hujufmodi fupplicationibus inclinati, Confraternitatem præfatam in Archiconfraternitatem, cum omnibus & fingulis prærogativis, Juribus, honoribus, & præeminentiis folitis, & confuetis auctoritate præfata tenore præfentium, fine cujufquam præjudicio, perpetuò pariter erigimus, & inftituimus: Ac infuper Archiconfraternitatis fic erectæ Officialibus, & Confratribus præfentibus, & futuris, ut ipfi alias quafcumque Confraternitates ejufdem Inftituti extra Urbem prædictam ubique locorum exiftentes eidem Archiconfraternitati, fervatâ tamen forma Conftitutionis rec. mem. Clementis PP. VIII. prædecefforis noftri defuper editæ aggregare, illifque omnes, & fingulas Indulgentias, & Peccatorum Remiffiones, ac pœnitentiarum Relaxationes ipfi Confraternitati fic in Archiconfraternitatem à Nobis erectæ, à Nobis conceffas communicare liberè, & licitè poffint, & valeant, auctoritate, & tenore præfatis fimiliter perpetuo concedimus, & indulgemus. Decernentes eafdem præfentes litteras femper firmas, validas, & efficaces exiftere, & fore, fuofque plenarios, & integros effectus fortiri, & obtinere, ac illis, ad quos fpectat, & pro tempore quandocumque fpectabit, in omnibus, & per omnia pleniffimè fuffragari, ficque in præmiffis per quofcumque Judices, Ordinarios & Delegatos, etiam Caufarum Palatii Apoftolici Auditores judicari, & definiri debere, ac irritum, & inane, fi fecus fuper his à quoquam quavis auctoritate fcienter, vel ignoranter contigerit attentari. Non obftantibus Conftitutionibus, & Ordinationibus Apoftolicis, & quatenus opus fit fupradictæ Confraternitatis aliifque quibufvis etiam juramento, confirmatione Apoftolica, vel quavis firmitate alia roboratis, ftatutis, & confuetudinibus, privilegiis quoque indultis, & litteris Apoftolicis in contrarium præmifforum quomodolibet conceffis, confirmatis, & innovatis. Quibus omnibus, & fingulis illorum tenores præfentibus pro plenè, & fufficienter expreffis, ac de verbo ad verbum infertis habentes, illis aliàs in fuo robore permanfuris, ad præmifforum effectum hac vice dumtaxat fpecialiter, & exprefsè, derogamus, cæterifque contrariis quibufcumque. Datum Romæ apud Sanctam Mariam Majorem fub Annulo Pifcatoris die VII. Martii MDCCXXXII. Pontificatus Noftri Anno Secundo.

F. Cardinalis Oliverius.

CLEMENS PAPA XII.

AD FUTURAM REI MEMORIAM.

CUm ficut accepimus in hâc Almâ Urbe noftrâ piè inftitutum fit, ut quatuor Confratres Archiconfraternitatis fub titulo Sacri Cordis Jefu in Ecclefia Sancti Theodori de eadem Urbe canonicé ut afferitur erectæ duo quidem manè, reliqui vero duo poft meridiem fufcipiant Officium feriâ fextâ cujuflibet hebdomadæ, fi ab aliquo fefto non fit impedita, fi vero fit impedita ad alium diem dilecti filii Prioris nunc, & pro tempore exiftentis dictæ Archiconfraternitatis benevifum quocumque tempore fivè in Hyeme inhorrefcente pluvia, ac Cœno, aut in æftivis caloribus facco, & fune induti, nudis pedibus, facieque contecta eleemofynas colligendi, quæ egenis familiis quolibet menfe diftribuuntur: Hinc eft quod Nos eorumdem Confratrum pietatem fpiritualium gratiarum, quarum Difpenfatores à Domino conftituti fumus, elargitione confovere, atque incitare cupientes, eifdem Confratribus prefentibus, & futuris, fi verè pœnitentes, & confeffi in unâ ex dictis feriis fextis cujuslibet Menfis per unumquemque ex dictis Confratribus ad fui Libitum eligendâ Sanctiffimum Euchariftiæ Sacramentum fumpferint, ac pro chriftianorum Principum concordiâ, hærefum extirpatione, ac Sanctæ Matris Ecclefiæ exaltatione pias ad Deum preces effuderint, plenariam femel dumtaxat quolibet anno omnium peccatorum fuorum Indulgentiam, & remiffionem mifericorditer in Domino concedimus: Infuper eifdem Confratribus verè pariter pœniten., & confeffis, ac Sacrâ Communione refectis in reliquis feriis fextis totius anni præmiffa peragentibus, &, ut præfertur, orantibus, feptem annos, & totidem quadragenas de injunctis eis, feu aliàs quomodolibet debitis pœnitentiis in formâ Ecclefiæ confuetâ relaxamus. Præfentibus perpetuis futuris temporibus valituris. Datum Romæ apud Sanctam Mariam Majorem, fub annulo Pifcatoris die XII. Junii MDCCXXXVI. Pontificatus Noftri Anno Sexto.

F. Cardinalis Oliverius.

THE DEVOTION TO THE SACRED HEART OF MARY.

AS the adorable Heart of Jesus was formed in the chaste Womb of the blessed Virgin, and of her Blood and Substance, so we cannot in a more proper and agreeable Manner shew our Devotion to the sacred Heart of the Son, than by deriving some Part of the said Devotion to the ever pure Heart of the Mother. For you have two Hearts here united in the most strict Alliance and tender Conformity of Sentiments, so that it is not in Nature to please the one without making yourself agreeable to the other, and acceptable to both. Go then, devout Client, go to the Heart of Jesus, but let your Way be thro' the Heart of Mary. The Sword of Grief, which pierced her Soul, opens you a Paſſage: enter by the Wound, Love has made; advance to the Heart of Jeſus, and reſt there even to Death itſelf. Preſume not to ſeparate and divide two Objects ſo intimately one or united together, but aſk Redreſs in all your Exigencies from the Heart of Jeſus, and aſk this Redreſs thro' the Heart of Mary.

This Form and Method of Worſhip is the Doctrine, and the very Spirit of God's Church: it is what ſhe teaches us in the unanimous Voice and Practice of the Faithful, who will by no Means that Jeſus and Mary ſhould be ſeparated from each other in our Prayers, Praiſes and Affections. This Conſideration has engaged the ſovereign Pontiffs and head Paſtors of the Church to give the Self-ſame Sanction to the pious Practices inſtituted in Honour of the ſacred Heart of Mary, as they give to thoſe of the adorable Heart of Jeſus both within their proper Limits. They both have equally their Aſſociations, and thoſe too equally enriched with the Treasures of the Church under the liberal Dispensation of its Governors. Many are the pious and virtuous Souls, who have drawn most signal Fruit, and Advantages from these Devotions.

Come then, hardened and inveterate Sinner, how great soever your Crimes may be! come and behold: Mary stretches out her Hand, opens her Breast to receive you. Tho' insensible to the great Concern of your Salvation, tho' unfortunately Proof against the most engaging Invitations and Inspirations of the holy Ghost, fling yourself at the Feet of this powerful Advocate. Her Throne, tho' so exalted, has nothing forbidding, nothing dreadful; her Heart is all Love, all Tenderness. If you have the least Remains of Confidence and Reliance on her Protection, doubt not she will carry you thro' her own most blessed Heart in the most speedy and most favourable Manner to the truly merciful and most sacred Heart of her Son Jesus.

THE ACT OF CONSECRATION TO THE SACRED HEART OF MARY.

O Holy Mother of God, glorious Queen of Heaven and Earth! I choose thee this Day for my Mother, my Queen and my Advocate at the Throne of thy divine Son. Accept the Offering, may it be irrevocable, I here make of my Heart. It never can be out of Danger, whilst at my Disposal; never secure, but in thy Hands.

N. B. This Feast has no fixed day. It is solemnized in some Churches with the Approbation of the Ordinary on the 8. of February, in others on the 1. of June, and in some Churches on the Sunday within the Octave of the Assumption.

Ye Choirs of Angels Witnesses of this my Oblation! bear me up in the Day of Judgment, and next to Jesus and Mary be ye propitious to me should the Enemy of my Salvation have any Claim upon me. Obtain for me at present the Gift of a true Repentance, and those Graces I may afterwards stand in need of for the gaining of Life everlasting. Amen.

THE LITANY.

Lord have Mercy on us.
Christ have Mercy on us.
Lord have Mercy on us.
Christ hear us.
Christ graciously hear us.
God the Father &c. *as above pag.* 31.
Heart of Mary, pray for us.
Heart of Mary according to the Heart of Jesus, pray for us.
Heart of Mary united to that of Jesus, pray for us.

Heart of Mary Organ of the holy Ghost,
Heart of Mary Sanctuary of the Divinity,
Heart of Mary Tabernacle of a God incarnate,
Heart of Mary always exempt from Sin,
Heart of Mary always full of Grace,
Heart of Mary blessed amongst all Hearts,
Heart of Mary illustrious Throne of Glory,
Heart of Mary Abyss and Prodigy of Humility,
Heart of Mary glorious Holocaust of divine Love,
Heart of Mary nailed to the Cross of Jesus,
Heart of Mary Comfort of the Afflicted,
Heart of Mary Refuge of Sinners,
Heart of Mary Hope of the Agonizing,
Heart of Mary Seat of Mercy,

} Pray for us.

Lamb of God, who takeſt away the Sins of the World, Spare us, O Lord.
Lamb of God, who takeſt away the Sins of the World, Hear us O Lord.
Lamb of God, who takeſt away the Sins of the World, Have Mercy on us.
℣. Pray for us O Holy Mother of God.
℟. That we may be made worthy of the Promiſes of Chriſt.

LET US PRAY.

Sweet Jeſus! who tenderly loveſt the moſt holy of Virgins, and art reciprocally moſt tenderly loved by her, grant, we beſeech thee, thro' the Interceſſion of thy moſt holy Mother, and by the Reſemblance her moſt holy Heart bore to thine, that we may ever return due Love and Affection for her Care and Tenderneſs in our Regard, who with the Father and holy Ghoſt liveſt and reigneſt World without End. Amen.

THE
REPARATION
OF
HONOUR.

MOther of God moſt worthy! whoſe Sanctity and ſublime Merit ſurpaſs the Comprehenſion even of the Angels themſelves, how great is the maternal Tenderneſs of thy Heart towards Mankind? How great thy Favours? How unworthy our Acknowledgment, our Gratitude, our Return? My very Soul is penetrated with Grief at the Conſideration of the many Injuries, thou receiveſt from Infidels and wicked Chriſtians by the Profanation of the Altars dedicated to thy Name, by the execrable Blaſphemies vomited out againſt thy maternal Virginity, Sanctity, and Integrity, but eſpecially from the Anguiſh, with which thoſe Sinners load thee, who heaping Sin upon Sin againſt thy divine Son, draw down Vengeance and Damnation on their own Souls; all which redound on thy tender Love and Compaſſion. Thus affected and upon this Conſideration, I fling myſelf at thy ſacred Feet, and tho' the greateſt of Sinners, moſt unworthy, and leaſt correſponding with the Graces I have received, I here enter my Proteſt againſt ſuch unwarrantable Proceedings, and beſeech thee, O Virgin more than Martyr, to accept the ſame, as a Reparation of Honour. Pardon my paſt Offences and Indignities, pardon thoſe of Mankind. Proſtrate in like Manner before thee, make us, Sinners as we are, ſenſible of the Favours thou haſt conferred upon us, and being truly contrite for the paſt, may we by thy Aid and Aſſiſtance, breaking the Chains of our former Thraldom and Slavery, live henceforward in thy Favour, and in the happy Liberty of the Children of God. May this our Act and Deed, O Saviour of the World, as we can do nothing more agreeable to thee, than to teſtify our Love and Gratitude to thy bleſſed Mother, may it, I say, be approved and confirmed by thy Blessing and Authority. Amen.

THE
SINNER'S ADDRESS
TO
OUR BLESSED LADY.

IT is to thee, holy Virgin, I have Recourse however unworthy of thy Goodness. I know thou never abandonest those, who call upon thee with Confidence, and that the Church does not call thee in vain the Refuge of Sinners: and this in Effect is the only Title, which is left me to dare to approach to thee, and shall I be so unfortunate as to be the first, and only one, that thou wilt refuse to hear?

Thou wilt find in me none of those amiable Marks, by which thou acknowledgest thy true Children. Slave of a shameful Sin, which tyrannises over me, I come to humbly beg thy Help to break my Chains.

Made sensible of the Beauty of a Virtue I have hitherto abhorred, I desire absolutely to quit a Vice, which has hitherto pleased me too much, tho' so highly shameful. Blessed Virgin! obtain for me the Grace to hate what I have loved, and to love what I have hated. Make my Eyes flow with Tears, that may efface all the Impurities of my Life. This Miracle is reserved to thee, O Mother of Mercy. Renew in me those Prodigies of Conversions, which thou hast formerly wrought, and appear now so seldom in an Age so corrupted as ours. The more miserable I am, the more proper Object I am of thy Compassion: nor can any Thing less than a Miracle free me from that infamous Passion, which has overruled me till now. This Miracle, O sacred Virgin, I beg of thee by that Purity, which made thee so agreeable to God, and which drew upon thee the Honour of being the Mother of his Son. Let not the Price of that Blood, which thou gavest to the Saviour of Men, be lost; refuse not to thyself the Plea-

Acts of Faith, Hope &c. 115
sure of reducing a straid Sheep to that heavenly Shepherd. Shew that thou art truly the Mother of Sinners, and let it not be said, that I perished at thy sacred Feet, where no one ever found but Grace and Salvation.

„ Many pious Books recommend the
„ following Prayer as very efficacious
„ for the obtaining Purity of Heart.

By thy sacred Virginity and immaculate Conception, O most pure Virgin, purify my Soul and Body in the Name of the Father &c.

An Act of Faith.

O My God! I firmly believe all the sacred Truths the Catholic Church believes and teaches, because thou hast revealed them, who neither canst deceive or be deceived.

An Act of Hope.

O My God! relying upon thy Goodness and Promises, I hope to obtain Pardon for my Sins and Life

H 4

everlasting, thro' the Merits of Jesus Christ, and by the Intercession of his blessed Mother and the Saints.

An Act of Love.

O My God! I love thee above all Things with my whole Heart and Soul, purely because thou art infinitely amiable and deserving of all Love; I love also my Neighbour as myself for the Love of thee; I forgive all that have injured me, and ask Pardon of all I have injured.

„ His Holiness Pope Benedict XIV.
„ observing how useful and even ne-
„ cessary the Acts of the three theolo-
„ gical Virtues, *Faith*, *Hope* and *Cha-*
„ *rity* are to eternal Salvation; in or-
„ der to excite all the Faithful of both
„ Sexes to the Exercise of these same
„ Acts, after having taken the Advice
„ of the sacred Congregation charged
„ with the Care of Indulgences and
„ holy Relicks, has most graciously
„ confirmed the Indulgences granted
„ by Benedict XIII. of pious Memory

Indulgences &c.

„ the 15. of January 1728. for the
„ aforesaid Acts. Viz.

„ 1. A Plenary Indulgence with
„ the Liberty of applying it to the
„ Souls of the Faithful departed, which
„ may be gained every Month by those,
„ who during that Space shall every
„ Day make the aforesaid Acts piously,
„ devoutly and from their Heart, pro-
„ vided that on the Day they would
„ gain it, the particular Time being
„ left to each ones Choice, being truly
„ penitent, and having received the
„ Sacraments of Penance and holy
„ Eucharist, they shall pray, as it
„ behoves, for Concord amongst
„ Christian Princes, the Extirpation
„ of Heresies, and the Exaltation of
„ our holy Mother the Church.

„ A Plenary Indulgence also at the
„ Hour of Death.

„ But to engage the Flock com-
„ mitted to his Charge to a frequent
„ Repetition of the above mentioned
„ Acts, his Holiness Benedict XIV.
„ has most liberally extended to each
„ Repetition, the Indulgence of seven

„ Years and of as many Quarantains
„ or forty Days, which may also be
„ applied to the Souls of the faithful
„ departed, and which his Predeceſſor
„ had granted but for once a Day.
„   Moreover his Holineſs has declared,
„ that all the aforeſaid Indulgences
„ ſhould not be annexed to the pro-
„ nouncing of certain determinate
„ Words, but that every one is at
„ Liberty to uſe any Form, provided
„ he expreſſes the proper Motive of
„ each of the three theological Vir-
„ tues. Given the 28. January 1756.
„ Signed *Fr. L. Card. Portocarrero*
„ Prefect. The Place of the Seal. *A.*
„ *E. Vicecomes* Secretary of the ſacred
„ Congregation of Indulgences.

THE
NIGHT PRAYERS.

„ Let us enter in Spirit into the
„ adorable Heart of Jeſus; let us
„ place ourſelves in the Preſence of
„ God; let us adore him, and give

Night Prayers. 119

„ him Thanks for all the Benefits we
„ have received from him particularly
„ this Day.

O My God! we adore thee thro' the sacred Heart of thy divine Son as our Creator and sovereign Good; we give thee Thanks for all thy Mercies to us spiritual and temporal, general and particular, but more especially for the Favours bestowed on us this Day. May thy holy Name be eternally praised and glorified, and may we never be ungrateful to thy Bounties. Amen.

„ LEt us ask of our Lord Jesus
„ Christ Grace to discover the
„ Sins, we have committed this Day,
„ and let us beg of him a true Sorrow
„ for them.

O My Lord Jesus Christ! Judge of the Living and the Dead, before whom we must one Day appear to give an exact Account of our whole Life, enlighten us, we beseech thee, and give us an humble and contrite

Heart, that we may see, wherein we have offended thy infinite Majesty, and judge ourselves now with such a just Severity, that then thou may'st judge us with Mercy and Clemency. Amen.

LEt us examine ourselves, and call to Mind the Sins we have committed this Day by Thought, Word, Deed or Omission; insisting particularly on the Failings we are most subject to.

PAUSE HERE A LITTLE WHILE.

MOst merciful Lord! we are sorry from the Bottom of our Hearts for all the Sins we have committed, purely because they are offensive to thee, who art a God of infinite Goodness; we sincerely detest them, and firmly purpose thro' thy holy Grace never to offend thee any more. Enlighten our Understanding, and strengthen our Will, that we may persevere in thy Favour till Death. Amen.

O My God! we firmly believe all the sacred Truths, the Catholic Church believes and teaches, because thou hast revealed them. Relying upon thy Goodness and Promises, we hope to obtain Pardon for our Sins, and Life everlasting thro' the Merits of Jesus Christ, and by the Intercession of his blessed Mother and all the Saints. We love thee above all Things with our whole Hearts and Souls purely for thyself, and we desire to love thee, as the Blessed do in Heaven: we also love our Neighbour for thy Sake, as we love ourselves, and we sincerely forgive all that have injured us, and ask Pardon of all we have injured. We adore all the Designs of thy divine Providence, resigning ourselves entirely to thy Will. We renounce the Devil with all his Works, the World with all its Pomps, and the Flesh with all its Temptations: we desire to be dissolved and be with Christ.

℣. Father into thy Hands I commend my Spirit. ℟. Sweet Jesus receive our Souls. ℣ May the blessed Virgin Mary,

S. Joseph, and all the Saints and Angels glorify, adore and love the sacred Heart of Jesus for us this Night, and pray for us to our Lord, that we may be preserved during it from all Sin and Evil.

Blessed Saint Michael defend us in the Day of Battle, that we may not be lost at the dreadful Judgement. O Angels of God, to whose Care we are committed by the supreme Clemency, enlighten, govern and defend us this Night from all Sin and Danger. Save us, O Lord! waking, and keep us sleeping, that we may watch with Christ and rest in Peace. Vouchsafe, O Lord! this Night to keep us without Sin. ℟. Have Mercy on us, O Lord! have Mercy on us: ℣. O Lord! hear our Prayer, ℟. And let our Supplication come unto thee.

LET US PRAY.

VIsit, we beseech thee, O Lord! this Habitation, and drive from it all the Snares of the Enemy. Let

Night Prayers. 123

thy holy Angels dwell therein to preferve us in Peace, and may thy Bleffing be upon us for ever thro' Jefus Chrift our Lord. Amen.

God the Father! blefs us; Jefus Chrift! defend and keep us; the Virtue of the Holy Ghoft enlighten and fanctify us this Night and for ever; and may the Souls of the faithful departed thro' the Mercy of God reft in Peace. Amen.

Imprimatur. A. van Tienevelt
Archid. Lib. Cenf.

Imprimatur. J. F. Diericx *Lib. Cenf. Reg.*

THE CONTENTS.

The Nature of this Devotion. Page	1
The Object of ditto.	6
The End of this Devotion.	9
The Advantages of it.	11
The Obstacles to it.	16
The Means of acquiring it.	17
In what it differs from that of the blessed Euch.	18
The Practice of this Devotion.	21
For every Year &c.	23
The Consecration to the sacred Heart.	28
The Prayer of S. Gertrude.	30
The Litany.	31
The Reparation of Honour.	36
Another for religious Persons.	40
The little Rosary.	44
A Practice for the Visits &c.	47
A Practice for holy Communion.	49
An Invitation to repair &c.	51
A Practice for religious Communities.	53
A Practice for a secular Family.	54
24 Acts of Adoration &c.	65
A Meditation for the Feast.	75
A Prayer for the Living and the Dead.	78
Pious Sentiments for every Day.	80
The Conclusion.	81
The Rules of the Association.	83
Letters Patent &c.	88
Three Briefs of Clement XII.	93
The Devotion to the sacred Heart of Mary.	104
The Consecration &c.	107
The Litany.	108
The Reparation of Honour.	111
A Prayer to beg Purity &c.	113
Acts of Faith, Hope and Charity.	115
Indulgences granted for ditto.	116
Night Prayers.	118

FINIS.

www.ingramcontent.com/pod-product-compliance
Lightning Source LLC
Chambersburg PA
CBHW022140160426
43197CB00009B/1361